How To...Read the Bible in Church

Bible in Church

A Training Course

Anna de Lange

Reader, Chaplain to Durham School

Liz Simpson

Priest-in-Charge, West Buckingham Benefice

GROVE BOOKS LIMITED

RIDLEY HALL RD   CAMBRIDGE   CB3 9HU

Contents

Acknowledgments
We would like to thank members of GROW for their ideas for this booklet, and especially
Christopher Byworth, Mark Earey and James Steven who commented on the draft text. Thanks
too to *Biblical Studies Bulletin* (distributed with the Grove Biblical Series), who gave us permission
to use ideas that originally appeared on its pages and on its online version accessible via the
Biblical Studies Bulletin web page on the Grove Books web site www.grovebooks.co.uk.

The Cover Illustration is by Peter Ashton

First Impression October 2003
ISSN 0144-1728
ISBN 1 85174 542 4

Introduction

1

As Christians we believe that the Bible is the word of God for us—his message to his people day by day and week by week.

Yet often the way we approach it in church does not reflect that high importance. The readings may sound boring, or they may hardly be audible, or be read without expression or understanding. Usually they are lifted out of context without explanation. In a culture conditioned by television to 'a picture with anything' they are totally word-based (whether heard, or seen on the page) and we are not helped to use our imagination or to respond to what is said. The word of God becomes just 'the reading' and fails to connect. What can be done?

The word of God becomes just 'the reading' and fails to connect

This booklet is for those who plan the reading of the Scriptures, who lead worship, and who actually read the word of God aloud in church. We hope it will help you understand and prepare for what you do as you read a Bible passage. It includes both background information that will help you to prepare to read and advice on the practicalities of speaking in church. As you read it, remember that your aim is always to help the congregation to understand what the reading means.

You might like to use the book and its questions in a group or as part of a course for the team who plan worship or the individuals who 'do the reading' in your church. There is space to scribble, so that you can make a note of the things that strike you as you read.

We hope that by considering the issues and ideas which follow, you will be inspired to think again about how the Bible is presented and read in your church and be helped to put across its message more effectively so that it can speak to people in a life-changing way.

2 Why Read the Bible in Church?

For Christians the Bible holds a unique place among the books of the world.

Through it God reveals himself to us, and communicates with us. That broad reason for reading it in church can be broken down into several smaller ones.

> *I wish that the Scriptures might be translated into all languages... I long that the farm-labourer might sing them as he follows his plough, the weaver hum them to the tune of his shuttle, the traveller beguile the weariness of his journey with their stories.*
> *(Erasmus)*

- To discover the Bible. For some people the readings in church may be their only (or their first) contact with God's word for them; we can no longer assume that every household reads or even owns a Bible.

- And then to get to know the Bible better, from a deep conviction that God teaches and equips us through it (Psalm 119.9, 11; 2 Timothy 3.16–17).

- To demonstrate that the Bible is the key book for Christians, binding us together as God's people with Jesus Christ as head.

- To tell the story of God's plan for his people, just as the children of Israel retell their story (such as Psalms 105–106).

- To keep us firm in the gospel truths, by reminding us of the historic faith. (2 Timothy 1.13–14).

- Enabling us to give good reason for our faith and back up our points with Scripture, just as Jesus did (1 Peter 3.15).

- So that we may learn from the mistakes of the past (1 Corinthians 10.11).

- It forms the basis of our liturgy. By reading the Bible, we find the passages that are reflected in our prayers, hymns and songs and thereby enrich our worship. For example: *O Lord, you have searched me out and known me...you discern my thoughts from afar* (Psalm 139) becomes

> Almighty God, to whom all hearts are open, all desires known, and from whom no secrets are hidden...

and Lamentations 3 v 22–23 ...*the Lord's compassions never fail. They are new every morning; great is your faithfulness* becomes the chorus of Thomas Chisholm's hymn:

> Great is thy faithfulness, great is thy faithfulness,
> Morning by morning new mercies I see....

- And because it has always been done. Jesus read the Scriptures in the synagogue (Luke 4.16–20), Paul told Timothy to read Scripture in public (1 Timothy 4.13) and Justin tells us that in early services the memoirs of the apostles were read for 'as long as time allows.'

If God's message is to be heard, it follows that the reading must be understood; to be understood it must be clear and vivid. On most occasions the translation used should accurately reflect the original Hebrew or Greek, although in some circumstances a good paraphrase or even a free rewriting (see chapter 3) can be helpful in making a story come alive.

To Think About

❏ Which of the reasons for hearing the Bible is important in your church?

❏ Have you got a good balance between word and sacrament? Or is the word either over-dominant (and maybe cerebral) or rushed (to get to 'the important bit')?

❏ Who is asked to 'do the readings' in your church?

❏ Many churches regard the readings as something that anyone can do, and so this ministry is one of the first that people are asked to join in with. Others believe that as we are listening to God's word for *us*, *now*, this is a privileged job, not to be taken on lightly. What is your church's policy? Might you consider setting up a team of readers?

3

How Do We Approach Bible Reading?

The Bible contains the story of God's dealing with the world.

It is also a collection of writings by different people, at different times and with different purposes. The way that we break the Bible up into small chunks (both in church and for our own Bible study) often means that we miss the wider sweep and context. To read it aloud well, we first need to see how the sorts of writing differ, and consider how best they might be communicated.

Many commentators divide the Bible into history, prophecy, law and poetry, but when we are thinking about reading aloud it may be more helpful to think of parallels with modern literature style.

- *News pages* Considerable parts of the Bible are in the form of narrative story, in the familiar style which we read in newspapers and factual books today. There is war reporting, social comment, politics, history, biography, obituary, and so on.

- *Stock market report* Some of the history is 'chronicled' in the form of a merely factual record. The basics, in a fairly indigestible form, give the essential information. Examples include the genealogies, large parts of Chronicles and Kings, and individual chapters such as Nehemiah 3.

> *Sometimes a Bible passage is more than one of these types of writing. For example, history might contain poetry, and the seven letters to the churches in Revelation 2–3 have elements of proclamation.*

- *A 'good read'* Sometimes an entire book of the Bible is more like a modern novel in form. It deals with history, but the story builds through the book and there is great emphasis on the human relationships as well as on the work of God. Examples include Job, Ruth and Jonah.

- *Oyez! Oyez!* The message of God is directly proclaimed by the mouth of an appointed spokesperson into a historical situation. It may be words of encouragement (such as Jeremiah 31) or of reproof (such as Hosea 4). The message is often introduced by words such as 'Thus saith the Lord' but might also occur without such an obvious signal. Proclamation is sometimes called prophecy, but it is not about the foretelling of the future (as modern ears might assume).

- **Short story** Short stories abound in the Bible, most obviously in Jesus' parables, or episodes like the healing of Naaman (2 Kings 5) that can be read in one 'bite.' Other passages express theological truth in story form, for example the stories of the Creation and the Fall.

- **Poetry** Parts of the Bible were written as poetry, though the form may have been lost in the translation we use. The books of Psalms and Lamentations quite clearly fall into this category (as religious poetry) as does the love poetry of Song of Songs. Other passages have a poetic structure, maybe with each verse beginning with a letter of the Hebrew alphabet, or with a repetitive beat such as that seen in the Beatitudes.

> *Lament disturbs the comfortable and comforts the disturbed*

- **Yours sincerely** The New Testament from Romans onwards consists mainly of letters written (often by being dictated to a scribe, or secretary) to encourage, correct and instruct the early church. In many of these, echoes of the writer's style—complete with afterthoughts and side issues —can be heard.

Implications

- Each of these forms needs a different style of reading. Consider yourself an actor on the stage: what tone of voice, what body language would you use if you were reading a letter aloud? Or reading a bedtime story, a thriller, or some poetry? There is nothing wrong (and a lot right!) with approaching reading in church in the same way.

- Sometimes we need long readings to be able to see the whole sweep of a story. Maybe we should be prepared to spend more of our worship time listening to the Bible.

When a book of the Bible is to be read continuously over several Sundays, you could mount a display giving some background information about it: when was it written, by whom and why? What was going on in the world at the time? Which other books of the Bible are contemporary with it? You could use maps and timelines to give some visual interest too. The notice sheet or church magazine can be another good way of giving people this sort of supporting information.

- Quite a lot of the Bible was written to be passed on orally rather than read. Sometimes it can be valuable to keep the pew Bibles firmly shut, and encourage people just to *listen* to the story. If the preacher wants them to follow the sermon in the Bible, then that is the moment to turn to the page.

- The Bible loses something if it is summarized or paraphrased, so accurate versions are needed for expository sermons and teaching. On the other hand in some circumstances (such as all-age Services) a paraphrase makes the story accessible to all.

- Some readings are only a few verses, and often need putting into context. Writing brief explanatory introductions is a skill which needs to be learned.

- The people of the Bible were people like us, and Scripture deals with potent human themes such as death, conflict and childlessness. We must expect and allow it to speak to people today. Sometimes the congregation will need time to absorb what they have heard, and leaving some silence, even a question to ponder, can be a useful device.

- The word of God is addressed to the world as well as to the church; there is an element of proclamation when it is read.

To Think About

❏ Should we sometimes choose the person to read the passage according to the type of writing? Some have gifts of dramatizing a narrative, others of reading poetry expressively.

❏ The proclamation of God's word requires a response. Should the Bible passages set the theme for the remainder of the service? If so, which reading (unless this is obvious because of the season)?

The Bible comes in many different types of translation, each of which can be useful in the right situation. These are the main kinds.

A **word-for-word** translation matches the original words with English ones. It is good at preserving the information in the text, so that historical fact and cultural context are transparent. This form is good for detailed Bible study or expository sermons. The Authorized Version (King James) is a word-for-word translation, though today's scholars have found better translations for some of the words. Modern ones include the New Revised Standard Version, which is used as the basis for Bible quotations in Common Worship. In the most rigorous word-for-word translations (such as in a Bible which puts Greek and English on alternate lines) the word order is also preserved so that the reader can see how individual words have been translated. This is helpful to the student, but difficult to read aloud.

A **thought-for-thought** translation seeks to create the same impact as the original, without necessarily using exactly equivalent words. So weights and measures might be rendered into metric equivalents, or colloquial sayings might be given in modern form. The focus is on the meaning rather than the words, but this can mean that some of the historical setting is lost. A thought-for-thought translation is often useful for helping people to see how the teaching might be applied to modern-day life. The New International Version and Contemporary English Version are of this type.

A **transcultural** translation goes a step further, by giving new equivalents for concepts that are meaningless to a particular set of readers —the lamb/shepherd image for Arctic peoples, for example. The cultural setting of the Bible is lost, but the meaning can be made more vivid. Transcultural translations are little used in Britain, although 'dialect' Bibles might come under this heading, and can make a familiar story come alive.

A **paraphrase** is a free thought-for-thought translation, but can also involve shortening the passage, as in a children's Bible, or expanding it for added clarity, as in the Living Bible. Paraphrases are useful for story-telling, and for all-age contexts.

Something else to look out for is **inclusive language**. Translations of the Bible that were made before about 1980 often use 'men' and 'brothers' to mean both men and women. Newer translations (or revisions of older ones) are sensitive to this, and will use other words or change the structure of the sentence. Check verses such as Matthew 4.19 ('fishers of men') or Romans 5.7 ('righteous man').

For more on this, see booklet B 3 *Translating the Bible* by R T France.

4 How are the Readings Chosen?

For centuries the Christian calendar has shaped the choice of readings for each Sunday, each festival, each day of the year.

Season by season the Christian story unfolds, and the events which shape our faith are retold. God's people are united in their worship by the Scripture that is being used, and the world's preoccupations can be challenged by eternal truth.

A lectionary is basically a cycle of readings linked to the Christian calendar and covering a wide range of Bible texts. Most use a combination of two approaches, according to the time of year:

- the first arranges the readings by season or theme related to the calendar, and is most used around the main festivals;

- the second follows one book of the Bible in consecutive, or nearly consecutive, passages so that the flow and story of Scripture is seen and we are taken into parts of the Bible that we might not choose to read.

There is another style in the sample lectionary modules found in *New Patterns for Worship* (Section C) where sets of readings suitable for sermon series on Bible characters, themes or stories can be found.

Sometimes the term 'lectionary' can mean a book with all the readings in the cycle printed out week by week and service by service. This sort of lectionary is produced in various Bible versions. The advantage of using one is that it makes it easy to look at all the readings together. The disadvantage is that it takes a 'chunk' of the Bible right out of its own context, and prints it with other passages which may give it another context and even change its apparent meaning. Therefore, even if you use a printed-out lectionary for the reading itself, it is always helpful to use a Bible when you are preparing, so that you can read the verses (or even chapters) that come before and after.

The Common Worship Lectionary

The lectionary year is divided into two types of 'season' (quite apart from the seasons of the Christian year)—what you might call 'open' time, and times when the readings are restricted to those in the authorized lectionary.

* The 'closed' time is basically around Advent/Christmas/Epiphany and Lent/Easter, and the authorized lectionary should be used for the principal service on Sundays.

* At other times alternative lectionaries, including the short modules in *New Patterns for Worship* or those constructed locally, may be used.

Readings and a psalm are given for three services each Sunday, following a three-year cycle. Most churches would probably use the readings for the Principal Service at the main (morning) act of worship, and those for the Second Service in the evening. At Holy Communion there must be a Gospel reading and at least one other (which may be Old or New Testament). A Service of the Word should preferably have two readings, but 'if occasion demands' there may be only one, and this does not have to come from the New Testament.

> *Is your pattern set in concrete? If the readings are very short, have more of them; if there is one very long one, consider breaking it into two or three, and spacing it through the service.*

Psalms

Many churches find using the psalms problematic, as the traditional Anglican practice of chanting them can be difficult for many congregations and even choirs. They rarely appear as a 'reading,' and may seem strange to our ears if they do. Yet they are a wonderful treasury of writing dealing with a wide span of human emotion and response to God, and we lose out on our Christian heritage if they are forgotten. So how can we use them in our worship?

There are various ways of saying or singing them in different styles, as traditional hymns, responsorial chants and songs, or 'worship songs.' Section D of *New Patterns for Worship* (pages 125–139) contains examples. Alternatively why not consider re-discovering them as Bible readings, to be read by one or more voices, just like the rest of the Bible?

To Think About

❏ Which readings are used in our church—lectionary or not? Who has made that decision? Should we make more of the permission to read other passages at certain times of year?

❏ How many readings do we have at each service? Are we regularly missing out on either the Old Testament or the Epistles?

❏ Do we use the Psalms? How could we help people engage with them and remember them?

Good Preparation

5

In what follows we assume that you have been asked to read, and have been told what the passage is, well before the service. If it is really necessary to read at short notice, do as much as you can!

Start with prayer It is an awesome responsibility to bring God's word to people, with the possibility that their lives will be changed by hearing it. Start your preparation by praying for yourself and for the listeners, that the word will come alive.

Which version? Then turn to the passage, using the version that you will read from. If there are Bibles in church for the congregation (or you print the readings on a notice sheet) it will be usual to read from the same translation so that people can follow the reading if they wish. Sometimes a preacher will want a particular translation because of a word or an emphasis that comes out more clearly, so don't change version from 'the usual' without asking.

If you don't have pew Bibles, or if you do but are using another version, you could consider:

- printing the passage in a news-sheet or service sheet;

- putting the words onto a screen using an overhead projector or a computer and data projector;

- encouraging people to listen (maybe with their eyes shut) to enter into the Bible experience.

Understand the passage You need to understand the passage yourself before you can communicate it to other people, so read it (and the verses that come before and after it) several times. If you need help, don't be afraid to ask the preacher or use a commentary, if you have one. Ask yourself what sort of writing it is and therefore what style of reading would suit it.

Check the difficult words Check and practise out loud any difficult pronunciations. Old Testament names can be a particular problem. If you haven't heard the name before a Bible dictionary might help, or you could ask the preacher. If all else fails, make a confident guess and go for it, being consistent if the name occurs more than once.

Expression Your speed and tone of voice lift the words off the page. Vary them according to what is happening in the reading. If people are hurrying, speed up; if they are puzzled, let that sound in your voice; let the wonder of what you are reading come through as if you had never heard the story before. Look for words to emphasize, and when a pause would help. You might find it helps to make pencil marks to remind you.

Now Give it a Go

Have a look at Exodus 17.1–7 in whatever version you use, and think about the human dynamics of the story. See it as an item on the news. What tones of voice would be heard? Maybe you might decide:

v 1   factual, quite slow—this is a long journey with pauses—but at the end there is a question: why camp where there is no water?

v 2   anger builds, and a union delegation visits the management. Moses is patiently reproving.

v 3   more anger, going back on previous decisions.

v 4   Moses reaches the end of his tether and cries out to God in fear of his life.

v 5–6 God calmly gives Moses the solution—and it *works!*

v 7   the aftermath; if your version does not explain the two names in the text (perhaps they are explained in a footnote) you might consider expanding the text to say 'Massah (that is, test) and Meribah (that is, quarrel).'

Beginnings and Endings

• Does the story need any introduction, or explanation of who it is about? If so, plan exactly what you are going to say and write it down. Your introduction does not need to tell people what the passage is about to say, but to put it into context for them. Ask yourself what they need to know in order to help them understand these words. For example, you might

Don't take the end of the story for granted —we may know that Egyptian army drowned in the Red Sea (Exodus 14), or that the Samaritan is the 'good guy' (Luke 10) but in the original circumstances these endings were a major shock.

want to say before a reading from Philippians that Paul wrote this letter to the Philippians while he was in prison. You can find out the basic facts from a commentary or Bible dictionary, but beware of stating disputed details as facts.

- If the passage starts with 'he,' 'they,' or some similar word, you might like to change it to make it clear who or what the passage is about. Write down the alteration.

- Make sure you know if any congregational response is used to introduce or close the reading. Write it down to be on the safe side.

- Post-it notes are useful to mark the beginning and end of the passage; you can write your introductory and closing words on them too.

In NRSV Luke 8.26 begins the story of the Gerasene demoniac. We have added questions in italics.

'Then [*when?*] they [*who?*] arrived at the country of the Gerasenes, which is opposite Galilee. As he [*who?*] stepped out on land [*out of what?*] a man of the city....'

By looking at what comes before this verse, it does not take long to make it clearer. For example:

◊ **by expansion:** *After Jesus had calmed a storm he and the disciples* arrived at the country of the Gerasenes, which is opposite Galilee. As Jesus stepped out *of the boat* on land a man of the city....

◊ **by abbreviation:** Jesus and his disciples arrived at the country of the Gerasenes, which is opposite Galilee. A man of the city....

Preparing your Script

If the passage is particularly difficult, consider typing or writing it out again in any way that makes it easier for you. This will further help you to understand the passage and work out how best to read it. You might decide to use a larger typeface and alter the line lengths so that they correspond to the natural rhythm of the passage. It is often helpful to take out the verse numbers as they obscure the flow—except that if you need to indicate that some verses have been left out, remember to make a note like 'and now continuing at verse 11' so that people who are following in their Bibles are not lost.

> You might mark up the first few verses of John's Gospel like this.
>
> In the beginning - was the <u>Word</u>
> and the Word was <u>with</u> God
> and the Word - <u>was</u> - God.
> He was in the beginning - with God.
> All things came into being - <u>through</u> him,
> and with<u>out</u> him not - one - thing came into being.
>
> Underlining reminds you to emphasize the word, and a dash to separate one word from the next, though with less of a pause than at the line break.

Practise—and Practise Again

Practise aloud, to get used to hearing your voice, and to what the volume and speed feel like. This differs with the size and layout of the building, with informality much harder to achieve in a large traditional church. It might help to go into church with a friend and ask him to stand at the very back and listen to you.

> *In music the object of practising is not so that you can play it right, but so that you **cannot** play it wrong.*

Can he hear clearly? Can he take in what you are saying? If there is a sound system, ask to practise with the microphone working before your first time and find out whether you need to turn it on and off.

By far the most common mistake is to speak too fast—and being nervous makes things worse. Listen to the pace of a 'good reader' at your church and see how slowly they take it. If you feel you are speaking at a snail's pace, it is probably about right. Remember to put in lots of expression as if you were telling a story to friends.

To Think About

❏ Which of these ideas are you going to apply next time you are asked to read in church?

❏ Practise applying the principles in this chapter to actual Bible readings. You might try these passages:

Deuteronomy 32.1–43 *Song of Moses*
Exodus 20.1–21 *Ten Commandments*
Nehemiah 3 *Jerusalem's walls rebuilt*
Luke 15.11–32 *The 'Prodigal Son'*
Romans 5.12–21 *Fairly typical Paul!*
Philippians 2.5–11 *Possibly an early hymn, now an Affirmation of Faith*

6 Making the Bible Come Alive

In some church services the best way of reading the Bible is as we have described in the last chapter—straight but well-prepared reading from the book.

But bearing in mind that many people today don't read books or listen to one voice speaking for very long and are used to a 'magazine' style of presentation, we may need to go further to make the words spring off the page and into people's imaginations.

As you grow in confidence, there are ideas in this chapter that you could consider. Obviously it depends on the sort of service, and the passage in question, as to whether they are suitable.

> *Sharing the reading with another voice can enhance the drama of prophecy or of a passage such as the Beatitudes.*

Using Mime or Tableau

> *Daniel 1 works well with a 'Whose Line Is It Anyway?' style mime line-up.*

If adapting a passage for full drama is too demanding for your resources, all is not lost. People find it easier to concentrate on a long passage if they can watch as well as listen. So assemble a team who will play out the action in silence, as the reading happens.

Dramatized Reading

There are many ways of dramatizing a reading. The best place to start is not with a book of dramatized readings or sketches but by engaging with the passage and seeing what it lends itself to.

- The usual way is to have one or more narrators with other voices taking the characters in the story. *The Dramatised Bible* is a good resource, but you can do the same yourself quite simply. It makes the flow of the drama better if you omit 'narrator' lines of the 'then Jesus said...and the Pharisee replied' type, as they should be clear from the dramatization.

Occasionally you might drop a moment of commentary into the reading. One reader, telling the 'walking on the water' story in Matthew 14, got to Peter's words 'If it is you, Lord, tell me to come out onto the water with you.' Then the reader looked up from the Bible and simply said, 'And regretted it immediately...' Everyone laughed—and the story came alive.[1]

- Take this further with passages that do not contain dialogue by looking at the style of the passage to see if it would be suitable for more than one voice. The Beatitudes could be read by two people to great effect (one voice saying 'blessed are...' and the other taking up 'for theirs...') as could any passage with an 'if—then' or 'you have heard—but I say' structure.

One church recently thought about consumerism (in an all-age service!) and read Isaiah 58.9a–14. They broke it into four voices, two reading the 'if' sections, and two reading the 'then' sections, the pairs on opposite sides of the chancel, starting their section in unison and then alternating phrases.[2]

- Another variation is to have different 'voices' coming from different parts of the building. God, for example, could be concealed in the pulpit or even in the vestry with his (or her!) voice amplified; a shout from the crowd can be just that.

- Involve the whole congregation, getting them to take parts such as the crowd in a narrative, or the angelic host at Christmas. Project the words onto a screen so that everyone can see them without having their heads in a book.

A different version of this is to invite specific spoken responses or sound effects to a particular word. Dave Hopwood's book Acting Up (see the list of resources) contains examples.

- If the passage has a lot of names or repeated words, prepare slips of paper with the words on (several slips for each one) and put them on seats before the service. Then ask people to listen for 'their' word, and when they hear it to stand, turn round, and sit down again (or some other action). Daniel 3, with the constant repetition of Shadrach, Meshach and Abednego as well as lists of musical instruments, is a good candidate for this treatment.

Making Mistakes

Especially when there are children present, you can encourage people to listen this way. Read the passage twice (not necessarily straight off, but with not *too* much of a gap between). The first time it is correct, but the second time you make mistakes—if they are amusing, topical or contrary to the spirit of the story, so much the better. You can offer points or a sweet to whoever spots the error. Can be noisy, but it is effective.

Reading from Memory

There might be people in your church who are gifted at learning passages *by* heart and then delivering them *from* the heart. Suppose the 'reader' were to come to the front of the church, look the congregation in the eye, and with no introduction start telling a story, or giving a message from God, or praising God in poetry. How long would it take people to realize they were listening to the Bible? It can be a show-stopping moment.

> I was asked to 'do something' with our first reading at our main Sunday service a couple of weeks ago. This is a time when the children and young people are still in, and the reading was Matthew 25.31–46, the sheep and the goats. It is a long reading, and I knew that the younger children would never sit through it. Something told me that I had to 'perform' it. I learnt the reading by heart the night before, and in the service I came to the front unannounced and simply started speaking. It took some time for people to realize this was the Bible readings until the end when I said 'This is the word of the Lord.' But it had a dramatic effect on me and on the congregation.
>
> First, it made me dig deep into the passage. There is nothing like learning it by heart to make you really reflect on what is going on, why words change (notice the change from 'Son of Man' to 'king' in v 34) and what they mean. In the course of learning it, I completely changed my mind as to what this passage is about!
>
> Second, it made me realize how easy it is to learn a passage, and how memorable Jesus' teaching was. There is a very clear structure which is repeated, with alteration, that makes it easy to recall. I have been brought up in a tradition where it was common to learn individual verses but why don't we learn passages more often?
>
> Third, when I started reciting the passage, everyone in the congregation was rapt, from the smallest to the oldest, for the whole thing. There was not a hint of restlessness. My six-year-old was even able to

point out where I had made a mistake, saying 'left' at one point where I should have said 'right.' It made me realize that our tradition of walking up to the lectern and opening the Bible actually turns people off—it is as if the routine of it dulls their expectation.

Fourth, we took the passage with its full seriousness. For this reading it is convenient that we have an aisle which actually divides the congregation into those on the left and those on the right. When I finished with 'This is the word of the Lord,' the response of thanks was noticeably muted, especially from the left (see verse 46)!

Next time you are faced with a narrative monologue, why not learn and perform it? You will never forget the experience![3]

Using Paraphrases or a Children's Bible

There are many books of Bible stories that give epic passages in a more digestible form. Some of the detail is lost, but an overview of the story means that there is the possibility of looking at all of it and its relevance to today.

Using Images and Sound

If you have the resources to project images, they can be very helpful in focusing on one part of the reading, or creating a 'mood' in which people may be more receptive to what the passage is saying to them, or showing some of the background of the text. You could use images of nature or abstract art portraying emotion with the psalms. A sequence of pictures of, for example, Galilee and fishermen could be used with gospel stories—an up-to-date equivalent of stained glass windows, teaching by pictures.

Using Video

If you are able to show video in church, it's worth looking at popularized versions of Bible stories such as 'Joseph and his Amazing Technicolor Dreamcoat,' 'Prince of Egypt' and 'The Miracle Maker.' They may miss some of the theological points, but they are familiar and visual, and can be used alongside some Bible verses or teaching. The *Testament* series of Old Testament stories are excellent and very faithful to the text.

Sound effects can be very effective, if used with care. For example, the passage from Ezekiel about the valley of the dry bones could be 'sounded,' if not by bones, by tapping wooden bars together, and the breath could be illustrated using wind chimes. Music can also intensify the point of the reading, either by following the passage or interspersing it with suitable songs, or by playing music in the background while the passage is being read. Take care, though, that any music does not make the reading inaudible, especially to people who do not hear very well.

> You might change the response (or at least its trigger line) to help the reading to 'hit home.' For example:
>
> ◊ Hear what the Spirit is saying to the church. **Thanks be to God.** (from New Zealand)
>
> ◊ A sung response, such as those from the Iona Community.
>
> ◊ One of the couplets given in the modules of readings in *New Patterns for Worship* (pages 107–123)
>
> Remember that the congregation need to know what to do and when. Write down the response, and make a note at the top of the reading to remind you to announce it.

Weaving Reading and Sermon Together

The rules for A Service of the Word (page 27 of the *Common Worship* main volume) give wide permission for varying the style of preaching. You can preach God's message in more ways than in a monologue from the pulpit, and some of these ways can take the form of an interactive reading.

- Work with a heckler—this is safest with a set script! Have someone in the congregation who leaps to their feet at intervals to interrupt the reading, asking questions that require an answer. The answer is given, and the reading resumes—until the next interruption.

Matthew 4.1–11 (with a heckler)[4]

Narr   Jesus was led by the Spirit into the desert to be tempted by the devil.

Heck   By the Spirit does it mean the Holy Spirit?

Narr   Yes, I think so.

Heck   Isn't that odd? I mean, the Holy Spirit, the ultimate goodie advisor, wants Jesus, the ultimate Goodie Hero, to be tempted! Temptation is bad and nasty, isn't it?

Narr   Not necessarily. The word we translate as tempted we could also translate as tested. A test is nasty if you're going to fail, but pretty good if it's going to show how good you are. If you're

---

really on top of things a hard exam is something you want, because it shows you really know it. So just think, tested rather than tempted. Anyway, after fasting for forty days and forty nights, he was hungry.

Heck I should think so too! It's bad enough giving up chocolate for forty days. All this Lent stuff is hard on the old self control isn't it? I bet Jesus was tempted to have a snack or two.

Narr Yes. The tempter came to him and said.....

• Intersperse songs, drama and teaching with the reading, giving a large part of the service a focus on the passage. This might feel frivolous, but in fact it can give the word of God the attention and time that it deserves. The story of Esther (in, say, three episodes based on the adaptation in *The Street Bible* by Rob Lacey) can provide a framework for a whole service. James Chatham's *Enacting the Word* (see resource section) has both worked-out examples and ideas for starters.

To Think About

Imagine that your theme for a service is to tell the story of Joseph's rise to power in Egypt, covering the events from his arrival until he becomes known to his brothers. One possibility is to read Genesis chapters 39 to 45 but not all the congregation will appreciate such a long monologue. Use the ideas in this chapter to plan how you might do it. There are some suggestions at the bottom of the page.

These are some of the possibilities:

• reading from a children's Bible
• singing one of the songs from 'Joseph and his Amazing Technicolor Dreamcoat'...
• ... or using a rap version
• miming the action: the stories of Joseph interpreting dreams (Genesis 40–41) work well, with the narration by one person while the action is played out by Pharaoh, the cup-bearer, the baker, and Joseph.
• dramatizing the reading, maybe in several scenes acted at intervals throughout the service. It then not only becomes the reading, but the entire structure and theme of the service, and can incorporate suitable songs and times of comment and reflection.
• playing a video—ask your local Christian bookshop, the library, or your local school, if they have one. The *Testament* video of Joseph is particularly good.

7

On The Day

All the prayer, planning and preparation that has gone into the reading so far is unseen; what you do on the day will make all the difference to the way it is heard.

The things you do from this chapter will be un-noticed if they go right, but will stop people listening if they act as a distraction.

- Where will you stand to read? In most cases it will be obvious, but if the reading is to be dramatized you may want to do things a bit differently. Remember that you must be heard by all the congregation, and should probably use the microphone if there is one, so that might restrict you.

- If you will be using the lectern Bible, put a bookmark in the page you need, or better still leave it open at the right place.

- Sit at the end of a row or where you can easily get to where you will be reading from.

- Make sure that you know where your reading comes in the service. If there is a hymn immediately before, go to your place during the last verse. Otherwise, relax and go with the style of the service.

- Allow the congregation to settle before you start speaking. This may take quite a while; watch to see when people are ready to listen.

- Announce the reading. If you want to encourage people to follow the reading in the church Bibles, give the page number first, then Bible book, chapter and verse. Just to confuse matters, some Bibles have separate pagination for the Old and New Testaments so you might have to make it clear that page 34 is in the

Be careful when announcing the book. Distinguish between John's gospel chapter 1 and 1 John (better to say John's first letter, chapter 1 in the latter case). And don't be too hasty to attribute letters to Paul. Hebrews may not be by Paul, notwithstanding what the King James Version says, and several of the other epistles were written by Paul *and* one or more of his companions.

back section of the Bibles if you are reading from the New Testament. Give people time to find it—this will take longer than you think—and watch to see when most are ready.

- Make sure you use your church's normal practice when announcing the Gospel reading, or be clear about when you expect people to join in the response. There are various ways of doing this, such as 'The reading is [on page xx of your pew Bibles and is] taken from the gospel of Matthew, Chapter 2 v 1–11. Hear the Gospel of our Lord Jesus Christ according to Matthew....' Or 'The gospel reading is printed in your news-sheets. Hear the Gospel of our Lord Jesus Christ according to Matthew....'

> *Standing for the gospel symbolizes the centrality of Christ to faith and Scripture.*

- Remember all that you have practised as you read the passage.

- When you reach the end, pause for a moment and look up at the congregation. Then say the words used to introduce any response, such as 'This is the word of the Lord.' Wait for the congregation to respond, then return without hurrying to your seat. The most common mistake with the closing response is for the reader to say the congregation's words instead of her own—leaving the congregation with nothing to say!

Making Your Voice Carry

Whatever part you are playing in the service, and however small you feel it to be, you play an important part in helping others to approach God. If no-one can hear what you say, then every word is utterly wasted.

The larger the building the slower you need to speak. When a church is full of people the sound is absorbed very easily and tends not to be heard clearly, so you have to take extra care. Here are some hints to help you.

- Unless you are reading from a lectern, hold your Bible and your head well up, so that you are looking out rather than down.

- Imagine that you are talking to someone right at the other end of the church. That way you will 'throw' your voice. If you don't know what this feels like, go into the empty church with a friend and hold a conversation with one of you at each end of the nave.

- Stand straight, well-balanced, feet apart, no shuffling. If you have your weight on your toes rather than your heels you will find breathing easier.

Using a Microphone

If there is a microphone, use it even if you have a loud voice. There may be an induction loop to help the hard-of-hearing, and some churches record parts of the service. In both cases the microphone is the pick-up for the system.

Microphones differ, so take guidance on the one in your church. However, some general principles usually apply:

- stand so that you are speaking towards (but not *at*) the microphone;

- normally there is no need to be closer than about two feet;

- ignore the fact that the microphone is there at all—it is there to reinforce your voice, not to do all the work for you;

- Microphones tend to 'flatten' the voice, so remember to make an extra effort to vary your tone.

If you speak as if you had no amplification, you will be doing fine.

To Think About

❏ How can we encourage softly-spoken people to project their voices?

❏ Should the people who read in our church be given a training session with the microphone?

Further Reading and Resources   8

About Lectionaries

Trevor Lloyd, Peter Moger, Jane Sinclair and Michael Vasey, *Introducing the New Lectionary: getting the Bible into worship* (Grove Worship booklet W 141)

The Christian Year: Calendar, Lectionary and Collects—the commentary at the back (Church House Publishing, 1997)

Lectionary Training Pack (Praxis, 1997)

Michael Perham, *Celebrate the Christian Story* (SPCK, 1997)

About the Bible in Worship

Michael Vasey, *Reading the Bible at the Eucharist* (Grove Worship booklet W 94)

New Patterns for Worship (Church House Publishing, 2002)—especially sections C (p99–123) and D (p125–156)

R T France, *Translating the Bible: Choosing and Using an English Version* (Grove Biblical booklet B 3)

About 'Ways of Doing it'

James O Chatham, *Enacting the Word* (Westminster: John Knox Press, 2002)

Dave Hopwood, *Acting Up* (National Society/Church House Publishing, 1995)

Rob Lacey, *The Street Bible* (HarperCollins, 2002)

Michael Perry (ed), *The Dramatised Bible* (Marshall Morgan and Scott/Bible Society, 1989)

Lance Pierson, *Storytelling* (Scripture Union, 1997)

Notes

1 Story told by Christopher Webb, Renewal Officer for the Church of Wales, in *Biblical Studies Bulletin 25* (September 2002).
2 Story told by Ian Paul in *Biblical Studies Bulletin* 24 (June 2002).
3 Story told by Ian Paul in *Biblical Studies Bulletin* 26 (December 2002).
4 Adaptation by Tony Ingleby. Full version accessible from the *Biblical Studies Bulletin* web page on the Grove web site www.grovebooks.co.uk (BSB 26).